Birds in Flight

Poems by Brenda Linkeman

Spartan
Press

Spartan Press

Kansas City, Missouri

Spartan
Press

Copyright © Brenda Linkeman, 2024

First Edition: 1 3 5 7 9 10 8 6 4 2

ISBN: 978-1-958182-71-0

LCCN: 2024937204

Cover design: SHU Press, Galisteo, NM

Title page image: Brenda Linkeman

Author photo: Salem Avenue Portraiture

Acknowledgments

The author would like to thank the editors of the following publications where some of these poems first appeared (in some form or another):

"SEAGULLS CIRCLE" first published as "MOIRAI" (*Strange Gods of the Prairie, The Gasconade Review,* 2021; *This Unexpected Life,* Spartan Press, 2022) and "GREEN BIRD" first published as "THE BOY AND THE PARAKEET" (*This Unexpected Life,* Spartan Press, 2022) "FRAIL BIRDS" first published as "PEN TO PAPER" (*This Unexpected Life,* Spartan Press, 2022)

I am very grateful for my cousin, Ed Epping, who read this collection and offered edits, insights, and invaluable guidance. And, to Dan Woodward, who has been a long-time encouragement to both my art, and to my poetry, in particular this collection.

Many thanks to SHU Press, Galisteo, NM for providing the cover design and illustration of the bluebird.

To my snowbird friend, Rebecca Shaffer – a sincere 'thank you' for allowing me to stay in your lovely condo in Soulard St. Louis while you were away in sunny Arizona. The space was an inspiration to write poetry in.

I appreciate all my wonderful friends, neighbors, and family members, who have encouraged me. And to all those who have followed my poetry posts on Facebook, thank you.

I will always be grateful for Mark McClane, Osage Arts Community, who opened the doors for me to publish.

Table of Contents

This collection of poetry is dedicated to the memory of my dad who loved bluebirds.

I found this verse he had written on a scrap of paper in the drawer of his nightstand.

Keep looking for the bluebird
And when you hear his song
Spring will soon come along

This collection begins with the ocean – a symbol of mystery, presence, and resilience. The poems then transition to the reality of inner cities, with their decay, dark side, and anxiety, followed by poems alluding to freedom and spirit. Finally, there is the awareness that seasons influence mood, and bring new beginnings. Spring, or 'tabula rasa', represents rebirth, or a clean slate. Throughout all the stages, places, and phases of life, almost invariably, there will be birds.

-Brenda Linkeman

AZURE SKIES

spiraling planet
ocean tides
coiling around
shifting sand
pools of salt water
seize azure skies
birds of all types
glide near unsettled shores
scattered
yet in
wild accord
a wide broad world
floating
a sole planet
spaces detached

UTOPIA BIRDS

crows
terra firma
black utopia birds
simple creatures
rooted in irony
contra
bold gulls
entitlement sense
then dependence
flowing through salt air
tiny sail boats
in water waves

BANTAM CROW

swells
waves of sea
sea gulls flowing
bantam crow
so out of place
ascends
aspires
into transformation
power animals
set free

BLACKBIRD

sky releases
shine
water ripples
join light
to form a
sea mist
that rises gently
blackbird
now
glides smoothly

GULLS

gulls watch
in an unselfish
display
calmly
guarding the seacoast
east and west

THERMAL SUN

thermal sun
beaches bare
crusty sand drifts
high walls
sandcastles
bleached
sea birds gliding
higher than salt water

SEAGULLS CIRCLE

a pink dawn lingers
she makes her way to the beach
tracing feather-like patterns of mice and snails
in the wet sand with her toes
wind blows over ocean waves
pausing long enough to become aware
of the warm water washing
first her ankles
then her knees
her feet reach for something solid underneath
with each wave she perceives a certain balance
and with each wave
more and more space washes away beneath her
her arms float
as if suspended by strings
threads attached to soft stars
seagulls circle with their curious heads
cocked to the side
soon they could be tangled in her floating hair
the distant horizon is dark violet
she breathes deeply of the salty air
and tastes the ocean
the shore becomes a life path

TIDE POOLS

seagull alone
reckless misty waves
lightly skimming
tide pools
diving
into splashes of salt water
so free
soaring
perpetually

TEARS BECOME SOUND

resolution
tears
become sound
acoustic sand
hot
free
sailing over waves
into the gale
seagulls glide
around

AUSCULTATING

auscultating
anxiety
flickering below
while seabirds
chatter
and clamor
at tides
and sand grains
crows
intelligent murder

BLUE LAYERS

time transformed
defunct itinerant winds
blue layers fading
New York
where there are
murmuring pigeons
in a flurry
still connecting
to
preoccupied
pedestrians

CLOUD SHADE

arriving wings
shield cloud shade
fluttering mass
rolls through currents
as gravity
denies their exit

SOLICITUDE

solicitude
continual
for years
healing ambitions
charades and mimicry
confrontation
by some wings
transcend

BARN SWALLOWS AND BEES

St. Louis South Side
the California Donut Company
will not re-open after all
gas pumping at the neighborhood 7-11
Dollar General plastic bags
float in a CO_2 breeze
the Big Four Chevrolet gone
Giuliani's Carnival Supply gone
buildings decayed
boarded up
there are 75,000 bees
located at the Jefferson Underground
and barn swallows – hundreds
though the sweet, machine fried
donuts are no more, and
newspapers cover the windows
still there is a neon sign
but it is dark
in this urban contrast
where swallows remain

DARKNESS DROWNS

calm life
paths in darkness
drown
the purpose
of light
in mystery
of sound
from wings
to peace

CLOUD OF BATS

San Diego
sometimes hushed
Mission Bay Drive
where neon pops flicker
around fast-food joints
empty coffee cups
swept into a gutter
glaring reflections and shadows
suppress doubt
as liquid black floods the night
thick as a cloud of bats
with the beach sand still hot
the salt air warm
just run
and imagine the sun returning

WEATHERED FEATHER

weathered feather
dazzling illusion
egg of discontent
hatching palter
fiction
sprigs and twigs
cracked open
it fell

ALABASTER PIGEONS

gray abyss
pale
departure
a loft of
alabaster pigeons
in swift flight
elapse
within
densest shadows

FEATHERED WARFARE

beveled emotions
grassy forests
reckless patience
chiseled oceans
risky refuge
feathered warfare
Iran meets West

WINGS CLIMBING

tense

mirrored vowels

wringing meanings out

uttering voice -

apprehension -

calm -

blameless -

wings climbing

explanations

arise in disorder

cease now

these rules

CITY PIGEONS - 1949

windows vacant
emotionless
ledges for city pigeons
the Alexian Brothers Hospital
in south St Louis
no longer exists
a lone church bell keeps time
on the next block
a distant time
when corridors thrived
and white shoed nurses
confidently
patrolled the halls

when the exorcism ended
the room was sealed off
the wing eventually demolished
and now
this neighborhood block
is hollow – empty
as if these buildings
ever had a soul

MURMURATION

ascending feather wings
clouds envelope
buffer
gliding murmuration
rolling through currents
defying gravity
denying exit
from a deep blue volume

DERELICT HEART

few prompts
hidden
in a derelict heart
boldness obscures
observation
dulcet fear
harbinger to nowhere
it was a sign of the time
sure and flawless
an outright struggle
scrub birds
no songs compete

CONCERNING TRIBES

misunderstanding
concerning tribes
lasting strife
freedom
long-fought life
now dormant
in transit
tolerating
untamed wings
locating
passageways

SINGLE FEATHER

single feather
halts
bird remains
in constant flight
echo's dim
distant
swirling flock
no refuge
asylum
or cover

DELUGE

another inspiration
lodged within
cerebral matter
spiraling into
streamlets
babbling into veins
once more truth
became well known
along this open path
birds came
floundering with deluge
others
they have flown

TRAGIC FRAILTIES

detached from
tragic frailties
wings support form
they soar
upon this place
so splendid
in isolation

ARRANGED CHAOS

plunging flights
encompass
light beams to thoughts
which filter like silt
into the mind
forever occurring
capturing plumage
sojourning
birds soaring
into a fine line
arranged chaos

WILD BLUE YONDER

diminished eyes
shelter convictions
free
in the firmament
and the
wild blue yonder
ungrounded
in bird flight

TOTEMIC MEMORIES

composed in soothing breezes
whisking leaves
and totemic memories
buried in former
adaptations
bringing fresh impressions
to the front
where sensory images remain
where seeds
from sounds - tones - notes
are planted in spirals of earth
lasting longer
than mirages of light
pausing for none except birds
understanding why
history is released
in keys - rests - clefs
into a vortex where all believed
once the calm scores were staged
purpose would be attained

CLOUD DANCE

reaching a lofty point
balance becomes transparent
aura is swift
brief glances
possible fluke
soaring and sailing
through clear air
into a cloud dance
nonchalant
joining spirit birds

ENDLESS VORTEX

green observance
ambiguous freedom
aspirations renewed
new beginnings
solitary
feathers
expand
into endless serenity
into cerulean
now an endless vortex
- spirit wings

SPIRIT BIRDS GLIDE

diminishing
reverence
of awe
conversely censure
without
veneration
inception
or beginning
spirit birds glide
thru
navy sky

LEMON TREE

potent currents
flora swaying
rhythm carries
concepts into a cloud space
answers become
- pastimes
- separate melodies
mist passing
minds snapping
in the lemon tree
alight
a robin
and a crow

GREEN BIRD

me with my fists on my hips
spying on a parakeet
through a front glass window
gazing into a home
at a small, green, emerald bird
she opened the cage
to show the bird could fly
it flew furiously around the room
when she opened the screen door
it brushed by my face
the boy on the horse
pulled on the reins
and we watched
the green bird fly away

SPARROW'S NEST

storms - sun
snow crystals
there's little need to doubt
all can see
doors lock from the inside
keys are often
found
in a sparrow's nest

PIGEONS STIRRED

pigeons stirred
supported
by ledges
wings pulled
into thin air
now
into a cool evening
uneasy
observing

SWEET TERPINOL FORESTS

passerine
flickering – twittering
wings flaying
perpetually
relentlessly
in search of
dense shrubs
sweet terpinol forests
sooner or later
nestling
content
in solitude

ARRHYTHMIA

perpetuate
acceptance
more
than a pair of wings
effortlessly
determined
to land
on the far side
of arrhythmia

BRIGHTLY FLOWN

brightly flown
circumstances
landing near
a dusty vase
a green stem
composed
from waters pure
touched by
chance

LUNA SELENE

aurora
leaves twist
luna selene
in a gust of wind
feathers float
words scatter
lines
compose
verse or
tanka

SWEET JAZZ

light is vivid
eyes expand
attention keen
regard flights
birds discern sentiment
mortal reactions
then susceptible
to sweet jazz
and fusion

FILLING ENVELOPES

symposium
free association
mass communication
filling envelopes
dropped
from
camouflaged wings
secured
by sentiment

BIRDS ARE BRISK

time is accelerated
fleeting
cabled
wire lines
birds are brisk
from the past
the future
has a beat

POSITIVE ENERGY

curtailed
diminished
night bloomers
begin seasonable actions
jasmine bird
fashions
creates and spreads
unfolded wings
accomplishing
identity affirmation
containing
positive energy

FRUITFUL BRANCHES

swift approaches
fog
where blackbirds cluster
in fruitful branches

FRAIL BIRDS

every little thing
to regain time
authored – penned
alluded to
- past insecurities
sounds spring up
lessons
like frail birds
legions of them
streaming
vast accounts
pen to paper
extricating
prompts

SOLITUDE EXPANDS

forget long silences
hushed moods
time pursuing
memories disguised by lies
truth emerging
solitude expands
conscious thoughts emanate
reversed partitions
walls of fate
wings migrating
emigrating

FRAGILE ILLUMINATIONS

seasons shift
revamping futures
consuming time
finding fragile
illuminations
escaping
to fly

YELLOW BEAKS

summers
lost
winging near
seasons sway
between ages
days and hours
concerning birds
with
yellow beaks

RED BLOOMS

hummingbirds
haven't flown south
they continue
zipping and sipping
around red blooms

TRANSCENDING

fall days
brisk
flying south
detainment
bright blue bird
ascending near
now a pair
a connection
renewal
between the living
and those
passed on
together
travelling
transcending

DARK PASSERINE

sojourning flocks anticipate trade winds
as they stream steadily toward the great circle
dark passerine collect on barren branches
or attach to thin suspended wires
then take flight over sterile fields
under a lingering sun
now fading in fire and warmth
ebony wings stretch in flawless unison
with entire masses risking this tedious flight
constantly spiraling
toward the deep, southern Elysium
surging on in urgency
perpetually in motion
these birds, they never tire
they soar on and on
with wings like sails
flapping through salt air
a thick miasma without edges
they swoop as tiny boats on the water waves
diving and splashing descending at last
as they reach their final shore

BLACK BIRDS AND JADE LEAVES

black birds and jade leaves
the abundance of autumn
fades

MATHEMATICAL SWARM

geese fly south today
it's a mathematical swarm
cold surrounds now

WINTERTIDE

passerine flurry
blue and ice
melting
clouds
branches reach
above
to nests
storing
acorns – walnuts – hickory
wintertide

A BIRD SPEEDS FAST

most seasons
relegate days
to sun and moon
when no light remains
no wind - no frost - no star
months will fade
within a greening vale
restoration
reinstitution
birds will speed on
mist lifts up to glide
floating - skimming
snowy mountain tops
cold triumphs

BLUEBIRD'S DEBUT

the bluebird's debut is today
breeze has released
gravity
now feathers light
push up into space

TABULA RASA

cells absorb sunlight
warmth
matching spring air
muted color
bird song
wings unfold
plants push up
once cold ground
joining alleviation
tabula rasa
wake the mind's eye
to new possibilities

Brenda Linkeman studied art at the University of Missouri in Columbia and completed her Bachelor of Fine Arts at the University of Texas in Arlington. Her collection of original bird paintings have been on exhibit twice at the "Audubon Center at Riverlands" in West Alton, Missouri. She began writing poetry when she was a sophomore in high school. Her poems have been featured in various publications including: The Trailor ParkQuarterly; The Gasconade Review's *"Wolf at the Door, Nobody Home"* and, *"Strange Gods of the Prairie."* Her first book of poetry, *"This Unexpected Life"* was published by Spartan Press in 2022.

This project was made possible, in part, by generous support from the Osage Arts Community.

Osage Arts Community provides temporary time, space and support for the creation of new artistic works in a retreat format, serving creative people of all kinds — visual artists, composers, poets, fiction and nonfiction writers. Located on a 152-acre farm in an isolated rural mountainside setting in Central Missouri and bordered by ¾ of a mile of the Gasconade River, OAC provides residencies to those working alone, as well as welcoming collaborative teams, offering living space and workspace in a country environment to emerging and mid-career artists. For more information, visit us at www.osageac.org

Osage Arts Community